WELSH STICK

Frontispiece: *This is the earliest representation of a Windsor chair. It is from a mid 12th century manuscript of the Laws of Hywel Dda. The picture is of a judge sitting on a chair. Note the tapered legs, arm rests and high back.*

WELSH
STICK CHAIRS

John Brown

246897531

WELSH STICK CHAIRS:

A Workshop Guide to the Windsor Chair

Library of Congress Cataloging-in-Publication Data

Brown, John, 1932-

Welsh stick chairs: a workshop guide to the Windsor chair / John Brown.

p. cm.

Originally published: Wales: Abercastle Publications, 1990.
Includes bibliographical references and index.

ISBN 0-941936-28-7 1. Furniture making. 2. Windsor chairs.
I. Title.

TT197.5.C45B76 1993

684.1'3-dc20   93-28897

CIP

ISBN 0-941936-28-7
Originally published by
Abercastle Publications, Wales, UK. 1990
Reprinted 1993
by
Linden Publishing Inc.
3845 N. Blackstone
Fresno, CA 93726

Printed in the United States of America

*Dedicated to the
memory of Laurence*

PLATE 1   St Fagans

This three-legged, pretty little chair has been called a weaver's chair. However, this is unlikely. A high stool is more appropriate at the loom. The chair would have been perfectly suitable for spinning, though is probably just a chair for general use. The hoop back is particularly delicate and interesting. Whoever built this chair had good skill and a good eye.

Author's Foreword

I have been advised by friends and colleagues, that, from the title, *Welsh Stick Chairs*, only an expert would understand what the book is about. Welsh Windsor chairs, on the other hand would be understood much more widely. Welsh Windsor chairs sounds to me like saying Welsh Scottish oatcakes, or Welsh Wexford glass. The chairs I am writing about are very definitely Welsh, and they are called stick chairs in Wales. They do, however, fulfil exactly the definition of what has come to be known, in Britain and the United States, as Windsor chairs. My judgement is to stay true to my original thoughts; only time will tell if I am mistaken.

There are people who do things, and there are people who write about things. If this book doesn't make sense it's because I prefer, and am happier, doing, than writing. Previous books on Windsor chairs, if they have referred to Welsh chairs at all, have called them English regional! Whatever else Wales might be, it is not an English region. It is offensive to Welshmen, or should be, to refer to it as such. So many facets of Welsh culture are entirely ignored. People often visit Wales for the wrong reasons. Ask a foreigner about Wales. He will tell of mountains, eisteddfodau, coal mines and Welsh dressers. There is so much more to Wales, and Welshmen would like to share it. I want to share with the reader my love of Welsh stick chairs.

I would have liked to have included much more about the history of these interesting chairs. But such information doesn't exist. There is hardly anything but the chairs themselves; they turn up in antique shops or museums with no provenance except the last place they came from. Many still exist in private hands. I feel a pang of disappointment when I see beautiful items in a museum. A museum is like a place of death, finality; this is how it was and now it is no more. But these chairs would look so undignified in a modernised farmhouse or a bungalow, that in this case the museum is the right place. And of all museums, St Fagans, the Welsh Folk Museum, is the best of all places for the Welsh stick chair. At St Fagans, amid thousands of treasures of Welsh rural life, the originals of some of the illustrations in this book can be seen in their correct setting. I spent a day with T. Alun Davies at St Fagans, and without his help this book would have been difficult to compile. I must thank him and his staff for photographs, which are acknowledged individually. The line drawings of chairs are the work of Owen Tudur Jones, and are published by kind permission of St Fagans. Gerald Oliver of Haverfordwest has written two interesting articles in the *Country Quest*. He has kindly given me permission to use the photographs from these articles, which were taken by Arthur Williamson, as also are the four portraits of my own chairs. Mr Oliver still has three of the chairs from the illustrations in his possession.

John and Lel Cleal of Workshop Wales, Fishguard, have been keen supporters of my work for several years, and I owe them a great debt for their encouragement over many lonely periods. In the village of Newport is a first-class bookshop owned by Tony and Eiry Lewis. They had the courage to buy one of the first chairs I made, and over the past ten years have always given freely their help and advice. Victor Wilkins showed patience beyond the line of duty in taking the set of photographs in my workshop. I would like to thank him. Finally, to the 400-odd people who have bought my chairs I also owe a word of thanks. It has been an act of faith on their behalf and I am rewarded beyond the financial recompense.

PLATE 2   St Fagans

A reconstruction of a Welsh fireside.

THE TRADITION
OF WELSH
STICK CHAIRS

PLATE 3

Board seat arm-chair of classic simplicity. The legs are hexagonal.

Cara Wallia Derelicta

Wales has been inhabited by Celtic peoples since 600 years before the birth of Christ. When the Romans came they found: "*This wild race of men, born of hard land, built of strong bone and mighty sinew, undaunted dreamers,*" or so reported a general, back to headquarters in Rome. With the final departure of the Romans, 400 years later, they left a pagan Celtic society. St David established the Christian faith in the 6th century, although a peculiarly Celtic brand. In the 8th century the Welsh church gave up its individuality, recognised the Roman calculation for Easter, disallowed its priests to marry (they didn't take this one on board until well after the 12th century), and altered their tonsure to conform.

The Norman conquest was the next great event in the history of Wales. It took only a few years to subdue England, Hereward the Wake being defeated in 1071. However, the Norman conquest of Wales was to take 200 years; and even then it was very tenuous.

Apart from the Celtic temperament, a key to the subsequent story of Wales really lies with one man: Giraldus Cambrensis, or Gerald the Welshman. It was Gerald's failure to achieve his lifelong ambition which has coloured the whole of Welsh history since the 12th century.

Gerald was only half Welsh. He was born at Manorbier in south Pembrokeshire in 1148, less than 100 years after his ancestors had landed at Hastings. Gerald's grandfather had married a beautiful Welsh princess, Nest. So his confusions can be understood. To be descended from the nobility of two proud, warring nations must have presented young Gerald with divided loyalties. All his life, to a greater or lesser degree, he was mistrusted by both sides. However, due to his education and training as a priest, his first call was to God, via the Pope.

His uncle had been Bishop of St Davids, the premier bishopric in Wales. In former times St Davids had had its own pallium, that is a direct line to the Pope. Now the Church of Wales was under the See of Canterbury. It had lost its independence due to the might of Norman arms.

Although Gerald spoke little Welsh — French and Latin were his languages — he was elected to the bishopric of St Davids, twice. Each time Henry II vetoed the appointment. Gerald was much too outspoken for the

English king and church. Furthermore, he would not swear allegiance to the English Archbishop. King and Church suspected that he would appeal to the Pope for the reinstatement of the Welsh pallium. Gerald made three trips to Rome, no mean feat in those days, to put his case personally to the Pope. He very nearly made it, but then, as now, politics is a messy business, and economic threats won the day.

Gerald was a broken man and retired to oblivion in Lincoln. He wrote several entertaining books, the most famous of which is the account of a journey through Wales when he acompanied Baldwin, Archbishop of Canterbury. The purpose of this trip was to gain recruits for the coming Crusade. Gerald's book includes many accounts of Welsh domestic life of the time.

Had Gerald won his case, had he become Archbishop of St Davids, separating the Welsh church from the English, the history of this nation could well have been very different. Nothing would have ever stopped the greedy Normans from over-running the country, but the circumstance of a single church, as in Ireland, would have had a unifying effect on the people, helping them eventually to win their independence. As Gerald said, "*The English fight for greed, the Welsh for freedom.*"

It is an interesting sidelight to know how the Norman English establishment saw the Welsh. King Henry II, writing to the Emperor at Constantinople said, "*. . . in a certain part of this island there is a people, called Welsh, so bold and ferocious that, when unarmed, they do not fear to encounter an armed force; . . . the beasts of the field over the whole face of the island became gentle, but these desperate men would not be tamed.*"

Owain Glyndŵr was the only other man who managed to make a serious bid for Welsh freedom. This was 200 years after Gerald, but by this time the damage had been done. The resources of the English could not be overcome. The intervening years of subjection had destroyed much of the spirit. There was no habit of unity.

The next 500 years represent the dark age of Wales. The upper-class abandoned its Welsh culture and anglicised itself. The people were impoverished and lived in small, scattered communities. Welsh folk were kept down by a repressive legal system, conducted in a foreign language. The law denied them any kind of equality, resulting in hardship, servitude and famine. It was never as bad as in Ireland, for Wales did not have the Catholic church, so hated by the English, but, nonetheless bad for all that.

PLATE 4

St Fagans

A well used, very comfortable arm-chair. The turnings are interesting. The massive arm, chopped and carved out of a solid piece of timber, is a real work of art.

The next great upheaval in Wales occurred at the end of the 18th century with the coming of the iron masters, followed by the coal magnates. This divided Wales more effectively than geography or church. Massive labour migrations into the valleys of south-east Wales occured, not only from the rest of the nation, but from England and Ireland, and even Italy. Until now the church had been that of the squire and the parson, the English church: *"You keep them poor, I'll keep them ignorant."* Here the great non-conformist wave found a ready congregation, hope in the life hereafter, even if there was little to be found in this one! The immediate result of the coming of the chapel was a vast increase in literacy, mainly through Sunday School teaching. This opium of the people was covertly and overtly encouraged by the masters and the politicians. Occasionally, the old Welsh spirit arose, as in the Merthyr rising of 1831, the Newport rebellion a few years later, and in rural Carmarthenshire, the Rebecca Riots. But mass nationalist discontent in Wales was all over bar the shouting. Apart from the miners, who have always fought their corner for better conditions, the last 100 years of growing liberalism and prosperity have introduced a pragmatism into Welshmen that never previously existed. The head says peace at any price, but in many the secret heart is sad.

A few dedicated men have never given up, and recently the Welsh Language Society has been able to recover some of the ground lost as a result of the 'Welsh Not'. The English still come to Wales to retire, or in search of a better life. Fortunately, the Welsh are tolerant people, for there is a tradition, in the presence of surly natives, for the English to exhibit a high degree of insensitivity when going about their daily lives. Our prince lives in England, and rarely visits his Principality; our Nation.

A coloured contour map easily shows that Wales is a hilly country. There is a central ridge from north-west to south-east; Snowdonia to the Plynlimon Range to the Brecknock Beacons. These hill peaks, averaging around 2000 feet, are surrounded by a high plateau of approximately 1200 feet. The high land has poor acid soil, for it is very wet. There are cracks of valleys interspersed throughout which carry the water away. Where the land gently slopes towards the coastal plains are areas more suited to limited types of agriculture. The main river valleys are very fertile, and most of the inland towns are situated on these rivers. Finally, there is the coastal plain, which in sheltered parts away from west-facing coasts, supports the best growing areas. Anglesey is traditionally the bread-basket of Wales, and in the south-east, which has good shelter, is the garden of Wales. Wales was de-forested quite early in its history, and there is little good timber. The best trees grow in the Marches bordering England. Travellers in the late 18th century pro-claimed the land as 'wild and romantic', they were not trying to make a living here! Tourism has been of ever increasing importance from that period until today and it is a vital part of the Welsh economy.

The period which concerns us is from around 1700 to the late 19th century. At this time, without railways or roads, about three-quarters of the country was inaccessible to any kind of heavy or bulky load. If it would not go on the back of a pack animal, it didn't go! If you add the poverty of centuries to this poor transportation there are two major effects on the lives of the small-holder, farmer and villager in inland Wales. The first is that the people in-dividually, and the villagers corporately, had to be self-sufficient in nearly everything. The second effect was that the people were not influenced by the fashions of their more urban contemporaries. If they made an object, whatever it was, a pot, a shawl, a spoon, an implement or a piece of furniture, the over-riding parameters of the design were availability of materials and fitness for use. This produced traditional and unique designs, from clothing to the con-struction of their dwellings. So the tradition accumulated which was unique to their particular area. Another area had another design.

With the passing of time, and increasing populations, men travelled to find work, or visited the coastal seaports, and in this way new ideas would come. In this atmosphere a type of Welsh furniture evolved, including the Welsh stick chair.

We take chairs for granted. Even the poorest people in the Western world have a few chairs in the house. In earliest times the chair was a symbol of power, a throne for the king, hung about with tapestries, a chair for the chief with the tribe at his feet. Even recently the best chair was father's, situated in a draught-free place near the range. The poorest people would have had no chairs at all. Probably the only furniture of an earth-floored hovel would have been some sort of chest. People did not have possessions, or very few. Every-thing then was hand-made by people, and was of value. The necessities of life were shelter, a fire and some cloth for clothes. Only very gradually did people acquire any goods. Human nature doesn't change and the possession of an oak table would have produced the same effect on a home as a modern fitted

PLATE 6   Author   PLATE 7   Author

Two particularly good examples of Welsh stick chairs. The comb on the right hand chair is interesting, for although it has no transverse curvature, the maker has tried to individualise this lusty chair with a shaped profile.

kitchen of the 1990s. So this gradual evolution, and the accumulation of cherished pieces, so regarded as to be entered, item by item, into the will or inventory of goods of a small-holder or farmer. Records from about 1650 show a yeoman of south Pembrokeshire listed as having *". . . stools, benches and a chair!"*

It all started with stools. Floors were rough, earth or perhaps slate, so these stools were three-legged to stand firmly on the uneven floor. Occasionally, one sees three-legged forms, a leg at each of the front corners, and a single leg in the middle rear. As the standard of living rose, so would be made for the head of the household a 'backstool' and we have what we know today as the Stick chair, or Windsor chair.

In prehistoric times the land of Wales was covered in Scots pine, but in the periods that concern us most, Welsh trees of timber size were oak and ash.

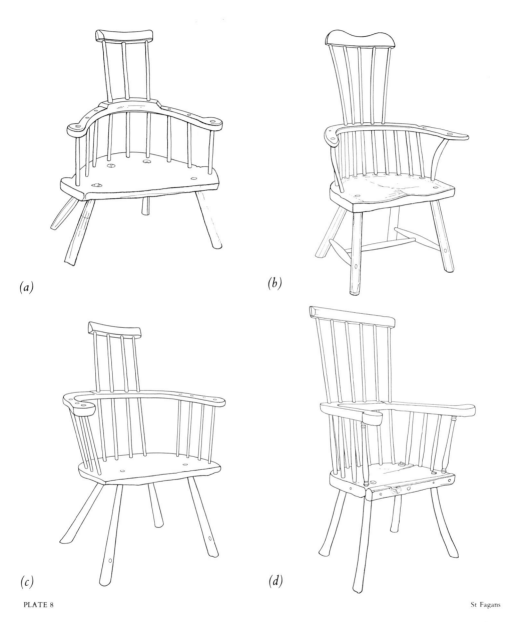

(a)

(b)

(c)

(d)

PLATE 8   St Fagans

(a) and (c) are examples of chairs which seem to come from mid to north Wales and have three or four heavy untapered sticks; (b) is a handsome chair with a slightly 'saddled' seat. Chair (d) has great charm, and has been 'modified'. The heavy arm and turned posts are interesting.

There was little use for pine or fir, even had it been available. These softwood trees require the power sawmill to make them useful. House frames were oak, and none other, as was most furniture. The only methods of converting tree trunks into usable timber were by splitting, then smoothing and shaping with an axe or adze, or sawing into boards over a sawpit. The sawpit entailed the labour of two highly-skilled men, one down in the pit, and the 'top sawyer'. With a saw six to eight feet in length they cut down the trunk to make planks. This was more often than not done on the site where the trees were cut down, as transporting heavy trunks would have been impossible. These boards were consequently expensive. On a good day a pair of sawyers could only do ten or twelve cuts.

Probably the first record of a back chair is in the manuscript of the laws of Hywel Dda (Howell the Good), a 10th century Welsh king. The surviving

PLATE 9   St Fagans

This fine trio represent the Welsh arm-chair. The right hand one epitomises the Welshness of these chairs. The difficulty of finding crooks of the desired bend means that the arm has less curve than we are accustomed to. However, with arms clinging to the sitter it is difficult to work on one's lap, knitting, sewing, etc. This could be a version of the lap chair, or nursing chair. The leg angles greatly enhance the rakish vigour of this chair.

PLATE 10   St Fagans

A four-square solid chair, obviously built to last. Some small attempt to scallop seat, even a slight hollow improves the comfort no end. Note the heavy arm and tapered sticks. The main arm posts are turned. The weak point is the legs; however, they are attractive, giving the chair its country appearance. A fine up-to-date undercarriage and this chair would be 'modernised' beyond recognition.

document, inscribed in the middle of the 12th century, has an illustration of a judge sitting on what is clearly a back or stick chair (*see frontispiece*).

The history of the English chair since about 1800 is well recorded. The first chair factories with division of labour were working during the Napoleonic Wars. There are no such records of the early Welsh chairs, or the late ones for that matter. The stick chair on this side of the Atlantic is a peasants' chair, of little value, and therefore not worth recording. Welsh stick chairs were not built by chair-makers, but almost certainly were the work of the village carpenter, wheelwright or coffin-maker. A house would be built by a group of people from the area, men of various skills who could afford the time. They were not builders as such. The trades were for the important things in life, the blacksmith and the wheelwright for agriculture. Household wares, such as furniture, were the luxuries of life which came after the provision of food. People had to do several things. A farmer might be a good hand at plastering, or the blacksmith's wife made candles. Furniture was made by men who were handy with tools. We see only the best of it, poorly made pieces have long since fallen apart. Many of the implements used on the farm had components of wood: plough beams, harrows, wheelbarrows, sleds and gates, and for economic reasons a good proportion of these would have been user-made.

Tracing the provenance of individual country chairs is a complicated business, probably with few exceptions, impossible. There is no scholarly standard work to refer to. Chairs with similar characteristics are found in different parts of the country (*Plate 14*). They cannot, with any certainty, be regionalised. Carmarthenshire, with large areas of good farming land and a

PLATE 11   Author   PLATE 12   Author

Two fine examples of north Wales chair type. The left hand example is quite primitive, with a heavy hewn seat. The right hand chair is altogether more skilful in execution, with a broad seat. However, they could well be from the same period, mid 18th century.

high proportion of better houses, is known for the quality and elegance of its locally-built furniture. Chairs found in the county, whilst unmistakably Welsh, have a greater sophistication than those made in the more remote parts further north (*Plate 20*). Dating Welsh stick chairs is very difficult. Whether these Carmarthenshire chairs were made concurrently with their more 'folk art' cousins from further north is difficult to say, but it looks as though they might have been. There is the possibility of another regional style. Some Welsh chairs have a wide lozenge-shaped seat, with only three or four untapered, heavier long sticks at the back. This type appears to come from the north (*Plate 8, a & c*).

As the standard of living improved, throughout Wales primitive furniture and chairs were made. By whom and for whom it is difficult to say. For certain, these items did not find their way into the squire's house and they were almost entirely rural. The one thing about the chairs is that they all fulfilled the strict definition of 'Windsor', in that they grew from a solid wooden seat, having legs and sticks socketed into that seat. The termination of the long back sticks was normally a comb, that is a piece of wood, sometimes curved, sometimes straight, into which the tops of the sticks were mortised. Rarely, a few later chairs have a steamed bow or hoop (*Plates 16 & 20*). Many of the chairs terminated at the arm, that is the rear sticks did not come up to the level of shoulders or head. These arm-chairs, quite common, are the forerunner of the smoker's bow or captain's chair (*Plate 14*).

What is it that makes these chairs so attractive that now they have become highly sought after collectors' items? Could it be some extension of the old Celtic art which makes them so appealing? — a naive folk art uncluttered by association with the contemporary urban styles. Many characteristics of the design are extremely good, and represent what we look for today in a well proportioned chair. The most obvious feature is that the legs are set well into the seat with a good rake. The English chair has the legs at the corners, and they are more upright. This is not so elegant. Stretchers to strengthen the legs were sometimes used; there seem to be no rules. When English goods and ideas reached the country village, the rural craftsman was influenced to use some design, and some of the chairs began to lose their spontaneity (*Plate 16*).

Rural poverty and religious bigotry have triggered much migration of Welsh people, mainly to the New World. In the 1670s, Quakers from Montgomeryshire and Meirionethshire were central to the formation of Pennsyl-

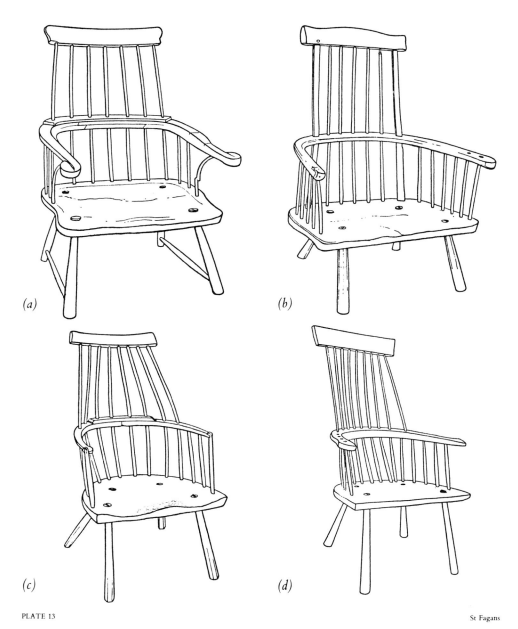

(a)

(b)

(c)

(d)

PLATE 13   St Fagans

Four chairs of character. In each one there is a different treatment of the 'bow in' of the sticks. All look comfortable to sit in. Compare with the illustrations on page 17 (b) & (d) where the sticks 'bow out'.

(a)

(b)

(c)

PLATE 14   St Fagans

"Pura Wallia . . ." These three arm-chairs are all of similar type: (a) is from Caernarvonshire; (b) from Cardiganshire, and (c) from Radnorshire. They represent a total Welshness from the mid 18th century.

vania. William Penn's deputy was a Welshman called Thomas Lloyd. Later came the 'Welsh Tract' and, in 1786, it was claimed that there were over 900 Welsh Baptist chapels in Pennsylvania and the adjoining states. Welsh ship-owners ran a continual service between Pennsylvania and Wales. From north Pembrokeshire and Cardiganshire large scale migrations took place to the Welsh Liberty settlement. Printing in the Welsh language went on in Penn-sylvania into this century.

Throughout the United States, Windsor chairs are much more widely seen than in Britain. Furthermore, they are to be found in the best parlours. The class distinction does not exist there. In court-houses and banqueting rooms, hotels and country clubs, American Windsors are in all the best places. There are many unique American-designed Windsors, and the industry or craft

PLATE 15   'Windsor Handbook'

The English chair. Wallace Nutting was very unkind about this chair. There are much worse shapes of English Windsor. This one is quite nice. Note the splat.

PLATE 16   'Windsor Handbook'

This chair illustrates what happens when a country-maker tries to copy his more sophis-ticated cousins. This is an English chair, made in Wales.

started in Pennsylvania. This in itself would not be important were it not for the fact that in two respects American Windsor chairs are similar to Welsh stick chairs. Firstly, there are no splats in the back of either sort. The splat is peculiar to English regional chairs and Wycombe chairs. Secondly, a common feature is the rake, or splay, of the legs. A collector of American chairs, the Reverend Wallace Nutting, wrote a book on the subject in 1917. He illustrates a bow-back English Windsor chair with a pierced splat (*Plate 15*). Under 'merit' he says, "*The English Windsors lack grace. Observe how stubby and shapeless the arms are. The bow is very heavy without being stronger for its purpose than a lighter one. The splat is peculiar to the English type. The legs are a very poor feature. They are too nearly vertical, and start too near the corner of the seat for strength or beauty, and their turnings are very clumsy . . .*" The oft repeated statement that American Windsors derive from the English chair could be in error. For historical reasons, and because of similarities in design, there seems to be a more direct link between the Welsh chair and the American Windsor. Perhaps the English version is the cousin, and the Welsh chair is the father!

There do not seem to be any records which can definitely be related to Windsor chairs in England before the 16th century. Here in Wales we have a record, in the form of an illustration dating to the mid-12th century (*see frontispiece*), so perhaps the Welsh chair is the 'Daddy' of them all! We have to remember that the Welsh language and literature predates the English by some 500 years, and that Welsh legal and social codes were relatively civilised when the behaviour of the English, especially the upper-class, was much nearer that of the jungle.

There is no proof, very little evidence of any kind, concerning the history of stick chairs, to prove these statements correct. But there are equally no facts available to disprove them. The circumstances outlined here must be seriously considered.

A parallel case exists in furniture decoration. There is a Welsh bible box which has a simple, roughly incised, floral scroll on its front. This is known to have been made in south Glamorgan or south Pembrokeshire. An American furniture expert would call this pattern Pennsylvania Dutch. There is a lot of furniture extant with this motive, the finer pieces having inlaid stringing. This could equally be described as Pennsylvania Welsh. When the Norman kings were having trouble with Welsh tribes, they imported and resettled into the southern coastal districts of Wales large numbers of Flemings. This is below

PLATE 17   Williamson

A pair of chairs from Carmarthenshire. It is difficult to date these chairs, but they are probably late 18th century. The saddled chair on the right is extremely good and shows many characteristics of an American type of chair of the early 19th century. This is the finest Welsh chair known to the author. In spite of an extremely heavy seat the chair has great elegance. The legs have restrained turnings and correct angle. The sticks have a subtle out-splay ending in a well shaped comb. The arm post carvings, the slight cut-away under the seat, and arm terminals, all combine to make this chair a fine example of the Welsh stick chair.

the Landsker line, which divides south Pembrokeshire, the English-speaking part, from the Welsh-speaking north. The principle of importing the Dutch was to form a barrier between safe Norman parts, and the unruly Princes of Deheubarth, now north Pembrokeshire, parts of Carmarthenshire, and Cardiganshire. So perhaps this form of decoration could be called Pennsylvania Dutch Welsh!

There seems to be a growing interest in Welsh chairs. Not so long ago many would have been smashed for firewood. Currently, they fetch a minimum of £500 at auction, and I have seen one sell at just under £4,000. It would be disappointing to think that this had to do with fashion. The true antiquarian has always appreciated these chairs. It would be nice to think that with more sophisticated taste, more educated views, it has become apparent that they are works of art, chair sculptures. The men who made them would be puzzled by this. Ananda Coomaraswamy said, "*An artist is not a special kind of man, but all men are special kind of artists.*" This certainly applied to the Welsh chair-makers. The chairs were, of course, somebody's prized possession. Some of them are not that strong and would have collapsed years ago were it not for the fact that

PLATE 18   'Windsor Handbook'   PLATE 19   'Windsor Handbook'

The two illustrations are from Wallace Nutting's 'A Windsor Handbook'. These chairs are from the same general period as the Carmarthenshire chairs.

PLATE 20   Williamson

A pair of chairs from Carmarthenshire, probably dating from the last quarter of the 18th century.

they were important to the owner. Can it be that we are just catching up in our asthetic judgements with these old craftsmen? Was he, like so many artists, just another sculptor ahead of his time.

When looking at these chairs it is well to remember the conditions under which they were made. Even the handyman of today has many more tools and devices than did the old Welsh craftsman. The wheelwright would, by the very nature of his complicated craft, have had a comprehensive set of tools. Many of his tools would have been village-made, forged by the blacksmith, and handled by the boy. These craftsmen would have probably had some land with a few sheep or a beast. It is more than probable that much village furniture was built by the wheelwright in his slack times.

A stick chair starts with a seat. The wheelwright might have an offcut of 'pit sawn' board, or perhaps there is a tree trunk to be cut up. This would be oak or ash. In the latter case a suitable length would be cut from the felled tree, and with axes and wedges our man would carefully make a split, then another split until he has a piece big enough for a chair seat 2″ or 3″ thick. The surfaces would be rough. He then smoothes the surface for the top with axe or adze, and to a lesser degree the seat bottom. It is rare to find these early chairs 'saddled', that is to say shaped to fit the human bottom, as all modern Windsors are. Occasionally, an attempt was made with a shallow hollowing, but it was obviously not considered important. The outline of the seat might be influenced by the shape of the wood he is using, it's all a matter of eye. Having finished the top, and taken off the loose grains of wood from the bottom, he would make the legs. These he splits roughly out of oak or ash and finishes with a drawknife. Often he would leave the legs hexagonal.

It is more than likely that he used a hand-turned auger for boring the leg holes. Iron braces, which we have today, were unknown, and the wooden variety, even when brass-bound, would have not been suitable for holes much over ½″ to ⅝″. The auger is similar to a modern carpenter's brace bit with a longer shaft on top of which was a metal eye through which a wooden handle would be placed to turn it. From past experience he would probably be willing to use an unseasoned seat, but the legs would have to be drier. If it is the wheel-wright making the chair, he would probably have pieces ready split out and seasoned for wheel spokes, and he would use them. Alternatively, the legs could be split from green wood and put up the 'chimney fawr' (large chimney), with the bacon and hams for a week or two. These legs, either three or four, would be banged home to the ready-shaped and bored seat, and wedged from the top. There would have been no glue used.

Hardly any steam-bent timbers were used in Welsh stick chairs. Some of the later chairs have steamed arms and bows but it was not common on country chairs. Most common was to make the arms of three pieces. One each side joined in the middle with a scarf joint, the third being to cover the short grains and the join at the back. Some, particularly the arm-chairs without a high back, had the arm carved out of a single piece (*Plate 4*). A bent branch or crook was used allowing the grain to run around parallel to the arm. So, with the three-piece arm assembled, joined with wooden pins or dowels, and the long and short sticks shaped, the chair would be put together. Often the comb was a straight piece of oak or ash. The subtleties of design were endless. Sometimes the sticks curved in, others splayed out. Often some of the long sticks were in two pieces. Each variation of hole spacing, each variation of curve between the seat, the arm and the comb, would have altered the character of the chair. Sometimes the sticks had slender tapers, others were heavy, up to ¾″ in diameter with no taper: a million variations. It is quite likely that for every chair in existence today, a hundred have disappeared, been burned, fallen to pieces, rotted in remote cowsheds, or just died of neglect.

PLATE 21   Andrew Edgar   PLATE 22   Andrew Edgar

These are two fine examples of present-day chair-making in New England. Michael Dunbar, who made these chairs, works in New Hampshire and has written several books on Windsor chairs.

MAKING WELSH
STICK CHAIRS

PLATE 23   Wilkins

This chair is made of oak and elm. I call it a Carmarthenshire chair, as it is derived from an old chair from that county. The doubling on the arm-back terminates in a 'swan neck'. This is seen on several old Welsh chairs.

"*Life without Industry is guilt, and Industry without Art is brutality*"

I came back to live in Wales in 1975. I had been made redundant and I was depressed. After years in a job I loved I had been told to go; my skills were no longer appropriate. I had been building wooden boat hulls for years, but now they needed men who could laminate plastics. Had I been prepared to don a plastic boiler suit, wear a respirator and work with nasty, sticky, smelly chemicals, I could have stayed. But I am an uncompromising woodman, I love it. My employers thought the adze as dead as a dodo, so they gave me a small handful of money and told me to pack my box. As I lived in a seaside resort there was not much work that I could do. I wasn't cut out for selling ice-creams, no killer instinct! My mortgage would be unpayable without a good job. There were plenty waiting to buy my house, so I sold.

I was seven-years-old when we moved from the safety of a large family in the valleys of Wales. Auntie was school-teaching in Kent, Dad came out of the pit and became a bricklayer. So, after a lifetime away, I returned to the 'Land of my Fathers'. What sort of a living could I make in Wales? There was plenty of building work, but I have a horror of the 'wet-trades'. I can only work in wood.

One day I saw a chair in the window of an antique shop in Lampeter. It was like a vision. I had never seen anything that had made so instant an impression on me. To my eyes this chair was beautiful. I had never had any interest in furniture or chairs. Like most people they were just the things you lived with. Now here was this lovely chair. I couldn't afford to buy it, but I could make one like it. Well, that is what I did. I made one. It took a long time. Chairs of simple form like the stick chair are surprisingly tricky to make. When you're building them you have to work from points in the air, angles of sticks, angles of legs; there are so many variables. Anyway, I was quite proud when I finished my chair. It looked alright. Of course, I wasn't able to put a century or two of patina on it. Now, twelve-years-old, it begins to look right. Family 'treatment' and a few thousand hours of bum polishing have done the trick!

At this stage I was interested enough to look for books on the subject. There are quite a few, both American and English. I still hadn't realised that what I had seen in that Lampeter shop was something quite rare and unique — a Welsh chair. *Then* it was just a Windsor chair. I went to museums. I visited High Wycombe where there is a museum devoted entirely to Windsor chairs. They have a very comprehensive selection of Wycombe factory chairs and English regional chairs. I don't think there were any Welsh chairs. The English chairs did not have the same spontaneity the same verve as their Welsh counterparts.

I enjoyed my youth. After the valleys I thought England was wonderful. The war started and we could not live in London, and through a series of events of which I have no knowledge, we ended up with a small-holding in the wilds of Kent. (There were wilds in Kent in those days!) We had no electricity, gas or sanitation, we grew much of our own food and kept chickens and a pig. We didn't realise it then, but we were living the 'Good Life'. We made few demands on the world's resources, and I was happy. So, as the Lampeter chair was one step towards my rehabilitation, the building of a tin shed in a field I bought, and a change to the simple life, completed my return. I live very happily without electricity or any other services. I have a workshop, a wood-stove and good health. There's a saying applied to yachts, which applies equally to life, "*Add lightness — and simplify.*"

A neighbour asked me to build him a chair like mine. I tried to — but it came out different. It was alright, but it wasn't the same chair. My neighbour was pleased. He has the chair now, he keeps it in the bookshop he owns. It then occurred to me that the reason for the diversity of pattern in the old Welsh chairs was that the makers did other things as well. They were not chair-makers as such, they were wheelwrights, coffin-makers, carpenters, even farmers. When there was need for a chair, somebody in the village made it, or they made their own. They didn't have patterns and jigs for continuous production. They had no consistent supply of uniform material. They used their eyes and their experience. It was like a sculptor doing his work, they 'thought' the chair, then they built their 'think'. Some of these chairs are a disaster to sit on, most uncomfortable, but they all have a kind of primitive beauty.

I now had the idea that maybe I could make a living out of building chairs. I loved making the first ones; it was new and exciting. But if I was going to be successful I had to try to get into the shoes of the old Welshmen who made these lovely chairs, and try to work as much like them as I could. It isn't possible to get very near it, life today is so different. I was convinced then, and even more so now, that the chairs were made as occasional items, and that none of them were made by chair-makers. Even with my small overheads, we do live in a total money economy — everything must pay. The lack of electricity has been a plus factor in my work. I have a strong back and don't care for bills.

I am impressed with the simplicity of old Welsh chairs. I have long been of the opinion that the work of 'fine' joiners, work with highly complicated joints, all hidden in the finished piece, leads to clean lines and continuous surfaces which make the finished work uninteresting. I am often tempted to ask these clever fellows *"and what's your next trick?"* The Arts and Crafts movement was responsible for a refreshing change. Ernest Gimson went to work with an English country chair-maker, Philip Clisset, to learn how to make simple chairs. Sidney Barnsley, working entirely alone, produced beautiful furniture with exposed dovetails; all the working showing. Of course, all this was over the head of the old Welsh craftsman. A great attraction of Welsh cottage furniture is its simplicity. So with the chair-makers, their work is the equivalent of naive painting. You hear people say *"a child could paint that."* Try it!

So I had first to unlearn, and then learn. I was lucky in the order that things happened to me. First, I built some chairs — then I got the books and found out how it should be done. By then I was conceited enough to think that I was closer to the men that built the chairs, 200 years ago, than the sophisticated authors. I have no intention of telling anyone how to build a stick chair, but I will tell you how *I* do it.

Before I go on to tell you about my methods of work, it would be well if I tell you a little more history of the Windsor chair. First a definition: What is a Windsor chair? Fundamental to a Windsor chair is a solid wooden seat; everything grows from this. From this seat the legs project down, and the sticks or laths project up. That's it. Arms, combs, fan-backs, balloon-backs, stretchers on the legs, different sorts of turning, a thousand variations — once a chair has a solid wooden seat with legs and sticks socketed into it, then it's a Windsor. The English Windsor started like the Welsh chair as a peasants' chair in the countryside. At the beginning of the 19th century, tycoons of the Industrial Revolution decided that what was good enough for Adam Smith's pins was good enough for the Windsor chair. They set up sweatshops in the Wycombe area of Buckinghamshire. The surrounding beechwoods of the Chiltern Hills provided the material for legs, sticks and bent parts, whilst elm for seats was plentiful everywhere. Bodgers with their pole lathes worked piece-work in the woods, turning legs and stretchers, which they sold to the factories on Saturday evenings. In the workshops, bottomers, benchmen and framers did the rest. Wages were poor and conditions appalling, and even in the last century strikes were not unknown. The owners of the factories were not chair-makers but money-makers. Design had a low priority, but the chairs had one major advantage — they were cheap!

Chairs were made at Wycombe — year in, year out — by the thousands. Piled high on horse-drawn wagons they were shipped to London. A month or so before making the journey most of the parts had been growing in the local woods.

Dealers bought these chairs and they were sold on to the less well off. They were bought for public houses, church halls and other places of entertainment. They found their way into the houses of the rich — but only for the people below stairs. Her Ladyship wouldn't be seen dead sitting in one. British class distinction at work, the chairs were cheap, so they were expendable. Like the herring, when kippered and rare, it was for the rich. When every fishing port had its smokehouse and they were cheap, then the poor could have them. When baked beans first came to England they could only be had at Fortnum and Masons!

There was no development on these cheap chairs. Identical designs on some types lasted for 150 years. These cheap chairs were exported all over the Empire (sometimes in knockdown form), and became known as the English Windsor. It beggars belief that there are today people making replicas of these chairs for sale in stripped pine shops. Fine cabinet-makers confined themselves to making joined chairs in the Sheraton and Chippendale styles. Some small Windsor chair-makers designed Windsor chairs with elaborate backs, highly carved splats, but used cabriole legs. These in many cases were very fine work, but a chair with cabriole legs is not, strictly speaking, a Windsor.

Building a Cardigan Chair

This name is arbitrary. I happen to live near Cardigan. Although I call this type of chair by a name, I can honestly say I have rarely built two identical. I prefer to build chairs first and sell them afterwards. This allows me to use the materials that I have to hand to the best advantage, and also gives me freedom, like an artist, to shape and style what I am doing. Frequently, until I have finished a seat, I have not decided the number of sticks, or the type of arm I am going to use. If I were to make to order I might as well be a factory. I can't always stick to this principle; when times are lean I'll build to order! I seldom measure much, although I do use patterns as a guide, varying them to achieve different effects. I bore most of the holes by eye, although for the legs I use bevels. The result of working this way is that I have failures, chairs that are wrong. You can't have it both ways, and this is better than reducing the job to its lowest common denominator.

PLATE 24   Williamson

A Cardigan chair in the showroom of Workshop Wales, Fishguard. This chair is rounded under the elm seat to take away the chunky look. The legs are made from straight-grained oak, as are the eighteen long and short sticks. The comb is cut out of solid elm in this case, although if I can find the right piece I prefer to use oak. Ash would do as well, and in this case could be steam-bent. The arm is steam-bent and is made from fast grown young ash which grows well in the valleys of west Wales.

Wilkins

1. General view of the workshop with an elm seat blank in the vice. I am cutting to a pencil line drawn round a pattern. This seat is 20″ across by 18″ deep, and it is 1¾″ thick. I do not generally use stretchers on the legs, especially if the seat is over, say, 1⅝″ and is from one piece of elm, and not glued up from several pieces. Immediately after the Dutch Elm Disease there was a glut of first-class elm. This has now been used up and it is increasingly difficult to find wide boards.

Wilkins

2. This is a turning saw in use. A wonderful tool to use. This one I made myself and the blade is a length of old band-saw blade. The blade is of the old sort which is sharpenable. Modern skip tooth, hard-tipped blades will not do. The grain on this seat is from side to side. I prefer it the other way, but it is not important in this case.

Wilkins

3. Having cut out the seat, the first job is to clean up the sawn edge. Here is a wooden jack-plane in use. I very rarely buy new tools. They are expensive and mostly made of cheese. A plane like the one I am using costs about £10, and the blades are thicker and made of much superior steel, either cast or laminated. Put an edge on that and it will last several times longer than a new iron for a modern plane. There are many good dealers who sell old tools. I often find interesting items on market stalls.

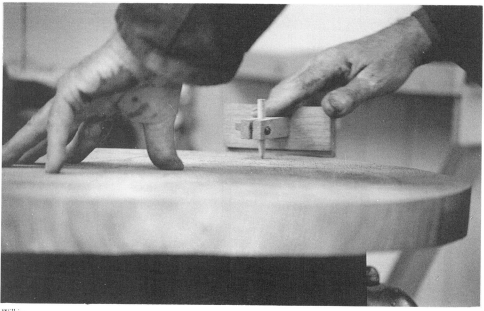

Wilkins

4. Having cleaned the seat up, I have to decide which is the top and bottom. Only experience can tell me this. What I am trying to do is to get a good 'picture' on the completed seat, a nice grain pattern. As it has to be scalloped out, this is not always easy to tell. I mark the top and bottom with a pencil line 2″ in from the edge. The marker gauge is a simple oak tool that one of my sons made many years ago.

Wilkins

5. A sculptor's adze in use to 'bottom' the seat. This is not a traditional way of doing this. I have and can use the full size gutter adze. However, if you look at the average dining–chair seat you will notice very gradual curves and probably a maximum depth of ½″, possibly only ⅜″. I like to cut in from my pencil line at a much sharper angle, and by using a small adze I can more easily control this. Also, I leave less to do with the finishing tools.

Wilkins

6. The small adze has a curve across the blade. It is used across the grain, and several passes must be made to achieve the right depth. All wood of the same species varies. An oak on a hill, in a valley, parkland oak, oak grown in windy conditions; they are all a bit different. None varies more then elm. Even a different part of the same tree can have totally different characteristics. I recall sailors talking about a 'soldiers' wind — blows both ways at once. Well, the grain in elm is similar. This is a nice piece and is behaving well.

Wilkins

7.   Chamfering the underside of the seat. This is one of the ways of taking the chunkiness out of the seat. Sometimes I round the bottom, some chairs I leave the edge at its original thickness, just taking off the arras top and bottom. All this is purely for appearance, and I go through phases, sometimes favouring one way, sometimes another. I have to do this part after chopping as otherwise the seat is difficult to hold in the vice.

Wilkins

8.   I screw a block of wood under the seat to hold it in the vice. The tool I am using here is a small 'round both ways' plane with handles. This again is a home-made tool. Chair-makers traditionally used travishers. Travishers are very hard to come by. I suspect this is because most of them are hanging neatly on the walls of the High Wycombe chair museum, or, because of their scarcity, are in collections. I abhor this situation; tools are for use. On the three visits I have made to the chair museum at Wycombe, I have been the only visitor, and I stand with mouth watering looking at literally dozens and dozens of travishers. Such is life. My tool works well, however.

Wilkins

9. The next stage in smoothing the seat. This is a scorp. It's a drawknife bent to a semi-circle and is really a cooper's tool. The scorp has a bevel on the outside, so it is reasonably easy to grind and sharpen. I find that for this work an engineer's vice bolted on top of the bench is essential. All the work is at a reasonable height, and my back does not suffer. I line the jaws with wooden blocks, and there is hardly a job in chair-making in which I do not use this vice.

Wilkins

10.   I decided to put a bead around this seat. I don't know why. It was quite unnecessary. I am using a block of wood with a screw protruding about $\frac{3}{8}''$. The edges of the screw head are filed sharp. Of 400 or so chairs I have built I have perhaps beaded a dozen. On this chair it looks alright, but it would have been just as alright without it. There's a lesson here somewhere.

Wilkins

11.   God forbid that I should ever have a fire in the workshop, but if I did, and had to get out in a hurry, I'd make sure my dumbscrape was in my pocket. This is a magical tool. Called a cabinet scraper in the tool catalogues, it is sharpened to have a wire edge with a burnisher of hard steel. It cuts like a plane — see the curly shavings on this seat. When they come from the shop they are oblong, square-sided. For this kind of work the edges need grinding to a gentle curve. It is a most pleasing business using a scraper.

Wilkins

12.   Ah, man's vanity! This is the signature I put on all my work. I did it. Well, I did part of it. I have a partner — the Great Chair-maker — so I put a cross, as we Celtic people see it. There is no point in smoothing the underside of the chair. It does not show unless the chair is turned upside down, and working with hand-tools only, one tends not to spend time on unnecessary things. Upon completion the rough part is sealed with black matt paint. I seal and polish the top, and if I did not seal the bottom as well there is an imbalance in absorbing air moisture and drying out. Unfortunately, with central heating from radiators so common, many of my chairs are cooked!

Wilkins

13.   Marking the position of the legs. This pattern is just a guide. Depending on the type of chair I am building I might move these holes in or out or diagonally before I actually bore them. Probably the appearance of the legs is the most critical part in making a good-looking chair. The holes in the pattern allow me to line up on the centre line pencilled on the seat bottom.

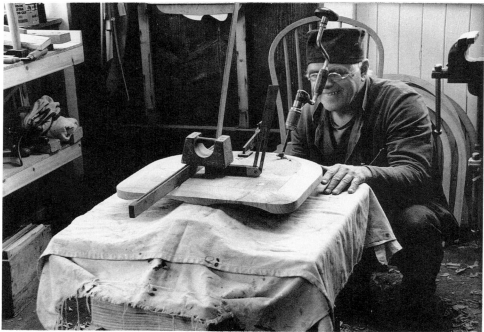

Wilkins

14.   Here I have cramped the seat upside down to a small stand made especially for the purpose. The two bevels are set at angles which I have marked on a pattern. The hole is 1¼″ and I am using a centre bit. Here you see me 'eyeing' it up. I bore the spiral screw of the bit into the seat until it is self-supporting. Just a few turns. Then I can move it a fraction to get it aligned as near as possible. I could make a jig for this, but then if I wanted to vary the angle I'd have to have another jig and so on. I like this way, it suits me.

Wilkins

15. More eyeballing! I hate to have anyone around when I am doing this job. It takes all my concentration. I even turn off the radio if I have it on. When I first started I had to scrap a few seats because I got it wrong. This is surely what David Pye means when he refers to the 'workmanship of risk' in his excellent book, *The Nature and Art of Workmanship*. I'm afraid if the telephone rings now it doesn't get answered!

Wilkins

16.   Having aligned the brace I then carefully stand up, place my feet apart and firmly grasp the brace so that it doesn't move. I then bore until the tip of the spiral can just be felt protruding through on the face side of the seat. I often think this must be a comical business, like the circus I expect to hear the drum-roll crescendo until finally I am through, can relax, and take the bow!

Wilkins

17. The centre bit does this job well. Traditionally chair-makers used spoon bits. If I did not bore right through this would be the best type of bit to use, as there is no lead screw, and one can therefore bore much closer without piercing the other side. However, I have never seen a spoon bit of this large size, and anyway I bore right through the seat. In this picture I have stopped boring and I'm feeling underneath for the point of the lead screw.

Wilkins

18. Having bored through from the bottom, the seat is now put in the vice. If I had bored right through from underneath the grain would have torn. This way we get a nice clean hole from both sides. Here is a clue to the use of elm for chair seats. I have now bored four holes for the legs through the seat. Yet to come are eighteen holes for the sticks. Each hole is a potential split in most woods, but not elm. This is why elm was used for wheel hubs, it is tough, and will not split.

Wilkins

19.   The legs are made of oak. Sometimes I make them of ash. Other woods with the same longitudinal strength would do. I make the legs 1¼″ square at the top to 1¾″ square at the bottom. In this picture I am planing the legs, first square, then hexagonal. I do this by eye; slight inaccuracies in dimension of the flats of the legs do not matter. The leg is held in a leg vice. This vice allows tapered pieces to be held firmly.

Wilkins

20. Here, the legs, which I always make a little oversize, are being rounded where they go into the seat. Before rounding, as the next picture shows, the cut is made into which a wedge will later be driven. This cut is done at this fitting stage so that when the final fit is made with the glue, the leg will not poke too far through the seat. Sometimes I round the leg for the whole of its length, sometimes to halfway, and at others I just round the top.

Wilkins

21. This little gents saw cuts the slot to just the right depth. At this dry fitting stage I hammer the legs in fairly hard. Notice that the leg holes in the seat are set well into the chair, and have a good splay. This looks well and is structurally superior to a leg at each corner. The surface of elm dents very easily, so I always have a piece of cloth between the bench and the seat.

Wilkins

22.   Banging the legs home. I have glued the legs, aligned the slots across the grain of the seat so that when I wedge there will be less tendency to split the grains of the seat apart. It is vital that the legs are bone dry. Wet timber would shrink and the legs would soon be loose. I also use dry elm for the seat, although if there is a little moisture when the seat dries, it shrinks around the hole, tightening the joint. Notice I have a piece of plastic between the seat and the cloth to catch the glue drips.

Wilkins

23. Hammering home the wedges. This job and knocking the legs in requires a brutal approach, and courage. I have split seats, particularly ones like this with a nice straight grain. However, these wedges must be hit home to the extent that they distort the seat. Mr Wilkins, who took these very fine photographs, had this chair in part-payment.

Wilkins

24.   This board is perfectly flat. I place it on the stand and level it. My floor is not accurate, so a slither of wedge here or there does the job. Behind me you will see the chair, legs and wedges all glued and knocked home tight. One leg is short, but it is still plenty long enough when they are all measured and cut.

Wilkins

25. Now, I place the chair on this board, which is dead level both ways. By using wedges and packing pieces I now level the chair from side to side. Light is a problem without electricity. In the winter natural light has gone by half past three to four. I try to work my year so that I can stop work at this time. If this is not possible I have paraffin lamps. Equally, in the summer I sometimes work until 10 p.m.

Wilkins

26.   I then put the level on the pommel and put my right hand fingers under the other end to find a level line fore and aft. My rule is two fingers for an arm-chair used for sitting only, and one finger plus a little bit for a chair which is to be used at a table or desk. This slope on the seat is vital. I have noticed many old chairs which have a level seat fore and aft. This gives the sitter the feeling that he is sliding off forward all the time. I get consistent feedback that the chairs I make are comfortable. Now, at this stage, the base is flat and level and the seat is at the correct angle.

Wilkins

27. I have found that an average comfortable height for the front of the chair from the floor is 18½″. Now I take a measurement from the blackboard to the tip of the pommel and deduct from this measurement 18½″. Say it measures 20¼″, well then, taking away 18½″ I know that the chair seat must lower 1¾″. On a thong of leather I have a collection of small squares of thin plywood, each a different width. I look for the one marked 1¾″, and using this I mark the bottom of each leg with a sharp pencil. This is where I must cut off the legs.

Wilkins

28.   Placing the chair as here, on a cloth to save marking the seat, I cut off the excess at the bottom of the legs. I hold the leg firmly, and sight any three lines. Then, keeping the saw accurate in two planes, i.e. down the length of the blade, and keeping the blade upright, that is not tilting it, I cut off the excess. You have to hold the body like an automaton. In this picture the leg nearest my face is already cut. I am sighting that cut end with the pencil mark on the lower leg nearest the camera, and as I saw, making sure the blade is aimed at that pencil mark, and that as I glance my eye down I can only see the back edge of the saw blade. It's all very exciting!

Wilkins

29.   The chair seat with its legs complete is placed to one side and I select an ash arm to shape up. I will describe the cutting and steaming process later. I cut the arm to length and, placing it in the vice, rough shape it with a surform. A coarse rasp would do just as well. There are several variations in the shape I can make. The ash starts at just under 1¼″ square. I can make the cross-section perfectly round or by taking off only a little at the corners I can have flats on top and underneath. I like to leave the ends square at this stage so that the finished arm has a slight swelling. After rough shaping I use my dumbscrape and finally sandpaper to finish the job. Ash can be worked to obtain a very high finish.

Wilkins

30.   There are eight long sticks and ten short ones in this chair. The short ones I cut to 10″, the long ones can be anything from 27″ to 36″. I start with ¾″ square section straight grained oak. First, I hexagon all the sticks with a jack-plane. Then I use a small metal block-plane to round them. The long sticks have a ⅝″ base, then a light swell to ⅝″, again at 10″ from the base, gently tapering to ½″ at the top where the comb will be. The shape of these sticks is very subtle but also important for the finished appearance of the chair. The short sticks go from a ⅝″ base to ½″ top with a slight swelling in the middle.

Wilkins

31.   This comb is cut out of solid oak 3″ thick. I am always looking for oak or elm of that thickness with a curved grain. The centres of the sticks on this chair are 2″ apart, so I am able to bore the eight holes before fitting. In fact, this is the first job I do on a comb. Occasionally, a piece will split whilst being bored, and I'd rather know before I have spent time shaping it up. Notice that I bore the holes at an angle. If I didn't, when it is fitted the middle would be lower than the ends, for bear in mind the sticks slope backwards. So by boring at an angle, when glued on, the bottom line of the comb is parallel with the floor.

Wilkins

32.   Here is the finished arm. First I mark the centre line. Then, having set
the dividers at 2″, I mark the through holes for the eight long sticks. I make
some arms out of solid oak or elm, that is not steam-bent, but cut to shape. In
this way I can make a much wider arm with swellings, or knuckles, at the ends.

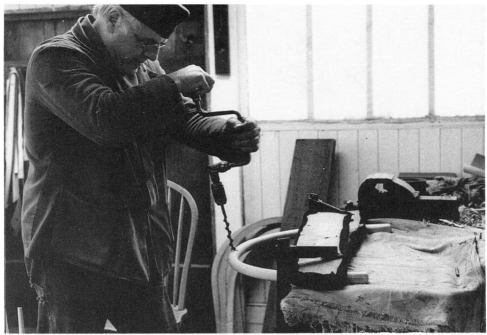

Wilkins

33. Boring the ⅝″ holes for the long sticks I do by eye. I more or less know the angle, so I stand in the right place, feet apart, and do not move until all eight holes are bored. I work through with a very sharp bit until the point of the lead screw can just be felt. Then I turn over the arm, re-cramp it to the bench, and complete the holes. I then mark the hole centres with the dividers for the short sticks, and bore them as far into the arm as I dare. This would be a good use for a spoon bit without a lead screw, but I've never got round to using one. It is important that all these holes are sharp and clean.

Wilkins

34 & 35.   Boring the seat holes is again done by eye. I make sure that I sit in the same position for all chairs, in this way I can vary the angles from a previous chair if I decide it is warranted. Sitting on a chair, with my feet gripping the two back legs to steady them, I bore the eight holes for the back sticks first. I have previously marked the positions with the dividers.

Wilkins

The short sticks are a little more complicated in that the front one has a little more angle, gradually decreasing towards the rear. Now, we have all the parts made, seat, legs, sticks, arm and comb and we are ready to glue up.

Wilkins

36 & 37.   Gluing up. Now is the moment of truth — is this to be a handsome chair? I use modern resin glue. There are a thousand glues on the market, all of them, I suspect, are good but you've got to be a boffin to find your way around them. I am an empiricist, I stick with what I know. However, I am willing to change if I see the results are better. Most modern glues are stronger than the wood they are gluing. I put plenty of glue on all the holes and on the ends of the sticks — and assemble.

Wilkins

Wilkins

38 & 39. The glue joints must be hammered home, without damaging the parts. This is vital as the sticks that enter the arm at the sides need special attention. I find that airlocks form, the joint, being a good fit to start with, is sealed airtight with the glue. Occasionally, I cannot overcome this without resorting to sash-cramps. Having got everything tight and washed off the excess glue, I then keep an eye on the chair for an hour. I have known the compressed air in the joints to push them apart!

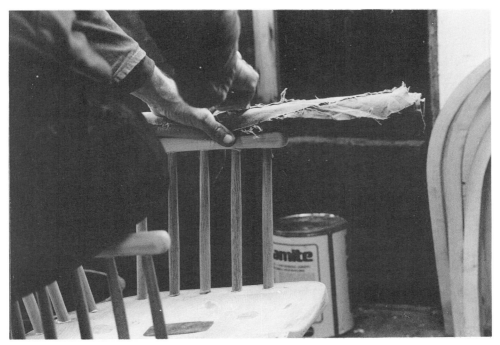

Wilkins

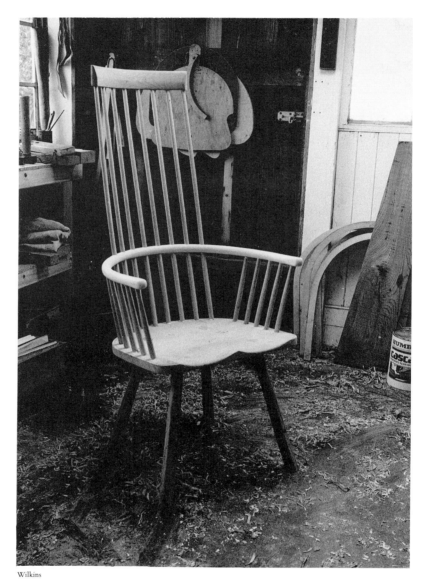

Wilkins

40.   The chair. All that remains for me to do is sand it. Washing off the glue with water raises the grain, so some 220 grit and 400 grit paper smooths it. Then I will seal it with sanding sealer and 400 grit paper it again. Finally, fine 0000 grade wire wool with a good quality wax polish will finish it.

Williamson

A Welsh arm-chair. The originals of this style of chair come from the north of Wales. Note the unusual seat shape and the solid wood arm. This chair is made entirely of elm. The sticks, which are not tapered, pass through the arm and seat and are wedged. This is a 'primitive' chair, but is my favourite. The example shown is stained dark green, then rubbed down and polished with brown wax, rubbing through the green in places. The effect is not meant to reproduce an antique finish, but to try to capture the 'Spirit of Wales'.

Bending Wood for Chair Parts

Not all wood is bendable, even with steaming. Undoubtedly, the best wood for this purpose is ash, and Welsh ash is the best of all. Young, fast grown trees are very good and they are plentiful. I have bent oak for arms and combs, but Welsh oak is not good, for it is too slow growing and the local variety is often knotted and gnarled. In England, beech is used a lot for bent parts, but I have no experience of this. I have always found beech too uninteresting in its grain patterns, but it is undoubtedly very tough and a worthy chair wood.

Traditionally, ash for arms was split out of a smallish log, say 8″ to 12″ in diameter, and perfectly straight. First, with axe and wedges, the log was halved, then quartered, and with a froe finally reduced until pieces which would encompass the size required were obtained. Then, in a shaving-horse with a drawknife, the arm would be shaped into a square ready for the steamer. All this is highly-skilled work, but very wasteful of timber. Times change. We must all conserve and utilise trees to the utmost.

I buy my freshly cut ash logs from a small local timber yard. The saw-mill is interesting in its own right, in that the young man who runs it, Quentin Davies, is the fourth generation in the family firm, James Davies of Abercych. (The yard is now actually at Cenarth on the main Cardigan road.) I quote from David Pye's book, 'The Nature and Art of Workmanship': "*The Welsh turner, James Davies of Abercych, told me that as a boy he had carved wooden spoons to be sold at fairs at, I think, twopence each. He said that at that price there was just time, when the spoon was finished, to look once at the inside, once at the outside, and then throw it over your shoulder on to the heap and start another! But having seen his work I do not doubt the spoons were a pleasure to look at.*"

Having bought my log from Quentin, he carefully saws it for me on his band-mill, making sure to keep parallel to the grain. We end up with the log sawn through and through at a thickness of 1¼″. Now the grains are all exposed. I am allowed to use the large Wadkin band-saw, and I now cut these planks into 1¼″ strips. If there is a slight bend in the grain I follow it so that I end up with a perfect square, 1¼″ × 1¼″, but perhaps with a slight curve, a very gentle banana shape. This is quite immaterial once it has been in the steamer.

Taking a log 10″ in diameter, 5′ long, and using my method of cutting I can get forty arms. Had I used the traditional splitting method I doubt whether I would have twenty.

I disagree with people who say wood should be partly seasoned for steaming. The best would be 'cut down yesterday, steam today'. Anyway, as soon as this ash is cut up it starts to dry. The moisture is sap. I drive it home and put it in a butt of water. Then I get my steamer rigged.

Two steamings a year supplies all the bends I need. My steamer consists of a 6′ length of heavy cast-iron pipe, 6″ internal diameter. At one end is a good fitting elm plug with a ½″ hole through it, in which is a copper tube. There is a wooden frame to support this end of the pipe and a pair of 'scissors'-type gallows to hold the other end. The copper pipe leads into a 2-gallon stainless steel tank. (The tank came from the inside of a liquid vending machine and it is a pressure vessel.) For heat I use a trusty primus stove. The open end of the pipe also has a plug with a handle on it. I also have a small ¼″ hole bored through this end with a removable wooden plug. I will explain why later. The whole pipe is lagged, sewn up in old rags and insulating material.

I start early on a steaming morning. Up at 6 a.m., fill the tank with water, light the primus. Everything must be ready and in its place, like an operating theatre. Forty ash sticks, pieces of string to tie round them so that I can pull them out, thick leather gloves, jigs for bending around, cramps, everyone I can lay my hands on, in fact no hold-ups. It's like the morning of the big fight!

I can get from five to seven pieces in the steamer, it depends how curved they are. Each piece has string which hangs down under the removable bung. Gradually, the whole contraption heats up. By lowering the outer end of the pipe I can drain off excess water, for until the pipe hots up, the first steam condenses. At this stage I leave the small bung, in the ¼″ hole that I mentioned, out. Soon, say by about 7.30 a.m., a small jet of steam comes out of this small hole and I know we have 'steam up'. The lagging of the pipe is so important. What is needed for bending is heat, wet, and pressure. Now I have worked out that if I remove the little plug from the ¼″ hole and the steam shoots out 6″ or so — I have pressure!

How long should I leave these pieces in? Difficult to say. About two hours is the norm, but I have left them too long when they get soggy and lose all the natural springy wood-like qualities. Really they want the minimum time that will allow them to bend. There are as many different theories as there are stars in the sky about bending wood with steam. What works for you! Meanwhile, I must prepare my jigs, and have a set of replacement ash blanks ready. I don't want visitors today!

My jigs are all sorts. The first one is a very fine piece of work. A 2″ piece of elm, looking not unlike a chair seat in outline, nailed to a larger piece of 2″ elm. Around the perimeter of the jig, and about 1½″ out from it, are ¾″ holes at 3″ intervals. The idea is to bend the arm around, putting ¾″ dowels into the holes, and then wedging the arm tight to the jig. It takes longer to write than it does to do! I have about four different shapes, and these determine the type of chairs I make. As the year goes on I judge what I will need. Some jigs are old seats that were too hard to chop. I bore slots at intervals about 2″ in from the edge. In making jigs I have to overstate the curve a little, for like all things natural, wood tends to want to go back to where it was.

9.30 a.m. approaches. Jigs are all ready, the first one cramped solidly to a bench. After all these years, the heart still beats faster. On with gloves. If ever the proverb 'make haste slowly' applied it is now. Out with the bung, a rush of steam. Pull the string you want, holding hot ash in one hand, replace the bung. Dispose of string and look for centre mark on arm. Now, place it on jig, bang in dowel, and wedge, ease round, no jerks, dowel and wedge, round, dowel and wedge, then the other side, round, dowel and wedge, round, dowel and wedge . . . it's there, o.k. . . . no split-outs. The tone is set for the day. And so it goes.

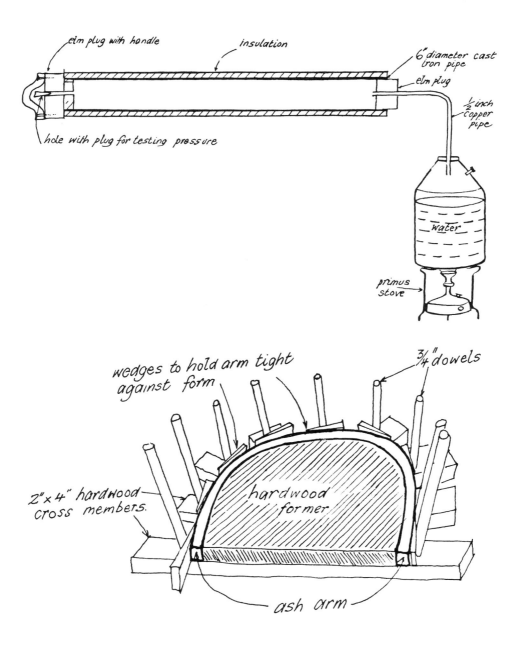

elm plug with handle

insulation

6" diameter cast iron pipe

elm plug

½ inch copper pipe

water

primus stove

hole with plug for testing pressure

wedges to hold arm tight against form

¾" dowels

2"x 4" hardwood cross members.

hardwood former

ash arm

Gear for steaming.

I have steamed six and had one good arm, I have steamed six and had six good arms. I could get masterful results by using a strap contraption. This is a method whereby a thin metal strap is clamped to the hot arm, and it is then bent round the jig. This requires more accuracy than I use. The pieces must be an exact length to fit in the end blocks of the strap. My main objection to this method is that if the arm is going to break or shred, better it happens now than when the chair is in use. Remember those lovely Thonet bentwood chairs? The wood for them was bent in huge numbers. Heated in an autoclave, and bent, dozens at a time in hydraulic presses. I have rarely seen one without a sheer brake, or incipient brake. Steaming is an art; science and technology cannot do it. Sometimes, having successfully bent an arm, I get the next piece out, put it on the jig, start to pull and realise this piece is not ready, although steamed for an identical time, and I put it back in the steamer.

I leave the arms on the jig for a couple of hours until the next lot in the steamer are ready. Then I release them and tie a cord across the open end to maintain the bend. Until they are cool and dry they will not maintain their shape. Steaming vastly accelerates the drying process. The sap is all out, and only water remains. The residual heat rapidly dries them. In one month they are totally dry.

Williamson

A Welsh library chair. This chair is made of elm. There is no taper on the sticks, they pass right through the seat and are wedged underneath. The wedges on the top of the arm are of black ash or ebony. This chair is sealed and waxed with no stain so that the natural figure of the elm is shown at its best.

Seasoning Wood in Wales

This is a contradiction in terms. Wales is a damp place. I'm glad it is. I went to Australia a few years ago, and a spell out there soon convinced me that our Welsh climate is much to be preferred. Things like trees grow here, grass and the garden. But seasoned wood is another thing. Should I decide to buy expensive kiln-dried oak from one of the big timber companies, by the time I had unloaded it from the lorry I suspect the moisture content would have doubled. My woodshed is only as dry as the surrounding atmosphere. Short of an insulated, heated building, I can think of no way out. I just have to do the best I can.

Top quality kiln-dried timber is very hard to find. I have bought such in the past, but even from large well-known companies there are air pockets inside the wood due to erratic drying. My experience has been such that I will no longer use any kiln-dried wood. I have elm which has been in my shed for four years. It must get damp in the winter and dry in the summer. I try to get enough inside about a year before I use it to finish it off. It's a very difficult subject. The problem is compounded because all my customers seem to have central heating. This in itself is alright providing the chairs are not stood right next to a source of heat. My word to my clients are, *"don't cook it for twelve months."* I suspect that this applies to most craftsman-built country furniture.

Conclusion

We are approaching the de-Industrial Revolution, or New Age. Empires disintegrate. Nations re-emerge. We must look back and see how it was done before, not to copy, but to learn. Some of us hope that Wales will again become a Nation. We must look at our history, and each of us in our way pluck something from it and revive it. How did my forefathers go about their life? What equipment did they possess? What was the spirit of the making? I have no doubt the word ecology was as strange to them as it was to me a few years ago (what is the Welsh for ecology?). They preserved their environment because they didn't have the monster tools to wreck it. No flails for them, they laid their hedges. Now I have the knowledge they didn't have and I try to preserve my environment. Science is destructive, it has wrecked the land, but only those old fundamentals, agriculture and handicrafts, can restore it.

We have come full circle. Good quality goods can be made as cheaply by hand as in a factory. The 'March of Time' has overtaken the tycoons. The costs of production, rent, rates, wages, holiday pay, maternity pay, insurances, and above all capital plant, have soared. The craftsman with small workshop, some good tools and a woodstove can compete. The industrialist's answer is to make nastier and cheaper goods, with less labour and more automation. People are beginning to despair about the rubbish; they want better and are willing to pay for better.

We are entering the age of the craftsman, where skills will be what matters. An age when the man who can grow asparagus will be more important than the man who can spell asparagus.

You may think that this is a long way from the Welsh stick chair, but I have plenty of time to think about things. I live in a beautiful place, I work at something I love, I make enough money to live, and my demands on the world's resources are very meagre. What is so unusual about this idyllic circumstance is that there is plenty of room for more to join.

Williamson

This is a Cardigan chair, similar in most respects to the one shown under construction. Note the difference in the style of the seat, there are no sharp demarcation lines, all edges are rounded. The back sticks are 33", which looks about right, and the top of the arm is 9½" above seat level. This is a comfy chair for an average person. The gallery shown here is at Workshop Wales, in Lower Town, Fishguard. John and Lel Cleal who run this lovely showroom have been instrumental in bringing my work to the attention of the public.

Bibliography

Abbott, M.: *Green Woodwork.* Guild of Master Craftsman Publications, 1989.

Alexander, John D.: *Make a Chair from a Tree.* Bell & Hyman, London, 1978.

Arnold, James: *The Shell Book of Country Crafts.* John Baker, London, 1968.

Blandford, P.: *Country Craft Tools.* David & Charles, 1974.

Comino, M.: *Gimson & the Barnsleys.* Evans Bros., London, 1980.

Coomaraswamy, Ananda: *The Bugbear of Literacy.* Perennial Books, 1949.

Crawford, Alan: *C. R. Ashbee.* Yale University Press, 1985.

Dunbar, Michael: *Antique Woodworking Tools.* Stobart & Son, 1979; *Windsor Chairmaking.* Hastings House, 1976; *Make a Windsor Chair.* Taunton Press, 1984.

Evans, Gwynfor: *Welsh Nation Builders.* Gomer Press, 1988.

Filbee, Marjorie: *Dictionary of Country Furniture.* The Connoisseur, London, 1977.

Fine Woodworking: High quality periodical. Books of extracted articles from above of interest to country craftsmen. The Taunton Press, Connecticut.

Gill, Eric: *A Holy Tradition of Working.* Golgonooza Press, Ipswich, 1983.

Hill, Jack: *The Complete Practical Book of Country Crafts.* David & Charles, 1979.

Hyde, H. A. & Harrison, S. G.: *Welsh Timber Trees.* The National Museum of Wales, 1937.

Hummel, Charles F., *With Hammer in Hand: The Dominy Craftsmen of East Hampton, New York.* Charlottesville: The University Press of Virginia, 1968.

Jenkins, J. Geraint: *Traditional Country Craftsmen.* Routledge & Kegan Paul, 1965.

John, Brian S.: *Rural Crafts of Wales.* Greencroft Books, 1976.

Jones, Anna M.: *The Rural Industries of England & Wales – Vol. 4: Wales.* E.P. Publishing, 1978.

Lambert, F.: *Tools & Devices for Coppice Crafts.* Distributed by the Centre for Alternative Technology, Machynlleth.

Langsner, Drew: *Country Woodcraft.* Rodale Press, Pennsylvania, 1978; *Green Woodworking.* Rodale Press, Pennsylvania, 1989.

Linnard, William: *Pit Sawing in Wales.* Folk Life, a Journal of Ethnological Studies, 1981.

Manners, J. E.: *Country Crafts Today.* David & Charles, 1974.

Maloof, Sam: *Sam Maloof, Woodworker.* Harper & Row, 1983.

Moser, Thomas: *Windsor Chairmaking.* Sterling Publishing Co., 1983.

Nakashima, George: *The Soul of a Tree.* Harper & Row, 1981.

Nutting, Wallace: *The Windsor Handbook.* Charles Tuttle Inc., Vermont. Orig. Publn., 1917.

Pye, David: *The Nature and Art of Workmanship.* Cambridge University Press, 1968.

Richter, Michael: *Giraldus Cambrensis.* National Library of Wales, 1976.

Rose, Walter: *The Village Carpenter.* A. & C. Black, London, 1937.

Salaman, R. A.: *Dictionary of Tools*. Geo., Allen & Unwin, 1975.

Seager, Elizabeth, (ed.): *The Countryman Book of Trades and Crafts*. David & Charles, 1978.

Seymour, John: *The Forgotton Arts*. National Trust & Dorling Kindersley, 1984.

Sparks, Ivan G.: *English Windsor Chairs*. Shire Publications, 1981; *The Windsor Chair*. Spur Books, 1975; *The English Country Chair*. Spur Books, 1973.

Sturt, George: *The Wheelwright's Shop*. Cambridge University Press, 1923.

Watson, Aldren A.: *Country Furniture*. New American Library, 1974.

Williams, Gwyn A.: *When Was Wales*. Penguin Books, 1985.

Yanagi, Soetsu: *The Unknown Craftsman*. Harper & Row;

and Ruskin on Hand Work;

and William Morris on anything.

Acknowledgements

The author and publisher wish to thank most kindly the following for allowing them the use of photographs and illustrations in this book:

Victor Wilkins of Llanfair Nantgwyn: photographs; Arthur Williamson: photographs; The Welsh Folk Museum, St Fagans: chair illustrations and photographs; Owen Tudur Jones: who actually did the St Fagans illustrations; Wynmor Owen: illustrations of steamer and jigs and tools; Charles E. Tuttle Co., Inc. Publisher: for the reproduction of three photographs from *A Windsor Handbook* by Wallace Nutting; two photographs from *Make a Windsor Chair* by Michael Dunbar. Used with permission of The Taunton Press, Inc., 63 South Main Street, Box 5506, Newtown, CT 06470-5506. 1984 The Taunton Press, Inc. All rights reserved.

Linden Publishing Co., Inc. are publishers and booksellers specializing in woodwork, metalwork and allied crafts. If you are not on our mailing list and would like to see our complete catalog write to:

The Publicity Manager

Linden Publishing Co., Inc.

3845 North Blackstone

Fresno, CA 93726

Phone toll free, U. S. and Canada

800-345-4447

Index